"A religion old or new, that stressed the magnificence of the universe as revealed by modern science, might be able to draw forth reserves of reverence and awe hardly tapped by the conventional faiths. Sooner or later, such a religion will emerge."

- Carl Sagan, Pale Blue Dot

4th Edition

Table of Contents

Preface

The Universal Life Church Ministries issues this book, the *Universal Life Church Ministries Guide to Divinity*, as a service to its ministers. In its capacity as the world's largest Internet-based ministry and the church which has ordained more people than any other church in history, the ULC Ministries as an interfaith not-for-profit organization strives to meet its ministers' demands for educational materials.

The Guide to Divinity will have two uses for the reader. As a primer, it will acquaint the reader with the major religious systems of the world by concisely surveying the doctrines of various faiths. Understanding the parallels between various religions might be the only way for one to learn what is unique about any one faith.

Throughout the life of the reader, the Guide to Divinity will serve as a reference text by means of which one may actually create intellectual links between various faiths. Religious fundamentalism can divide people from their own neighbors and breed ignorance and strife, preventing dialogue between cultures. The ULC Ministries makes as its goal the promotion of interaction between various religions, the recognition of their compatibility, and the free exchange of ideas to the end that each faith tradition can benefit humankind.

Please keep in mind that this book reflects the research and personal experiences of various people and all of the ideas and concepts therein are debatable. Ultimately, the sections on individual faith traditions serve as summaries of the most common or popular beliefs of a given faith's practitioners. When writing this book, it was important to us that each section be acceptable to the majority of members of its described faith, with secondary approval coming from persons outside of the faith being described. Anyone who disagrees with a claim set forth in this book is welcome to make a statement on the Internet forums of the ULC Ministries where every opinion has a voice.

Introduction

The Universal Life Church Ministries invites each of its ministers to define religious terms as they see fit, but for the practical purposes of this guide we shall provide the following working definitions.

"Religion," as ULC Ministries defines it, is a method by which a sentient entity can bring out some profound beneficial change. The ULC Ministries prefers this definition to all others because it encompasses all world religions as well as most other less prominent faith systems. One interpretation of this definition is that all religions have a way of recognizing the following:

- Humankind at large has some flaw.
- This flaw makes all who possess it unsatisfied.
- The flaw is the only cause of dissatisfaction.
- A specific faith system is a way to relieve suffering incurred from this flaw.

(Please note that while many definitions of religion will cover major world religions, this particular definition also respectfully applies to non-spiritual faith systems such as atheism.)

THE UNIVERSAL LIFE
CHURCH MINISTRIES

Guide to Divinity

4th Edition

African Traditional & Diasporic Religion

Introduction

African traditional religions are those practiced by the original inhabitants of Africa and can be divided into four different groups: the Nilo-Saharan, the Niger-Congo, the Khoisan and the Afro-Asiatic Religious Traditions. African diasporic religions, however, are those that developed when African traditional religions practiced by African slaves in New World regions like the southern United States, Latin America, and the Caribbean Islands were mixed with other religions being practiced in these regions at the time.

History

There are many different traditional and diasporic religions, and each has its own history and origin. Among traditional religions, for example, one Nilo-Saharan group was monotheistic, while another was non-theistic (as were the Khoisan groups). The Niger-Congo group, moreover, was concerned with the manifestation of spirit in nature, while the Afro-Asiatic group was henotheistic; that is to say that they focus worship on one of many deities in the belief system. As sub-Saharan slaves were brought to the New World, they often merged their traditional religion with the predominant non-African religion of their New World region, such as Catholicism, Kardecist Spiritism or Native American traditional mythology.

Different people have been responsible for influencing the development of the various traditional and diasporic religions. In the Yoruba traditional religion, for instance, one of the present leaders in the faith is Prince (Babalawo) Adigun Osolun, who also serves as high priest of several other sects, including Oke, Egbe and Obatala. Another example is the influence that Marie Laveau and her daughter had on the development of the diasporic religion Vodou in 19th-century New Orleans.

Reach & Spirituality

Taken together, traditional and diasporic religions have been designated as a "major religious group" and are believed to have approximately 100 million adherents worldwide. Approximately 45% of the people living in Africa today are followers of traditional religions, although this figure may be significantly higher as some of those who are deemed adherents to Islam also follow Yoruban traditional religion. Diasporic religions are also still extensively practiced today in the southern United States as well as Central and South America.

How basic religious concepts are defined in African traditional and diasporic religions also differs from religion to religion. The diasporic language of Winti as practiced in Suriname, for instance, is based on a belief in the personification of supernatural spirits, while followers of Yoruban traditional religion believe that it is the manifest destiny of all human beings to merge with the divine creator.

Agnosticism, Atheism and Non-religion

Phi, the Golden Mean

Introduction

Agnosticism is the commitment to material science and strict mathematical logic as being the only sources for knowledge on the nature of existence. It can be paired with any other number of religious beliefs at the user's discretion.

This is strictly distinct from atheism, which takes the added step of believing that the lack of evidence for an intelligent spiritual force indicates that no such thing exists. There are some atheists who believe that while nothing intelligent exists in the spiritual realm, there is a spiritual realm nonetheless; these people are pantheists. A few people think nothing of spirituality at all; this group might be called non-religious.

Agnosticism

Belief in spirits almost always includes a belief that the spiritual realm and the physical realm will, on occasion, interact with each other. A person who looks for evidence of the interaction is an agnostic; if the evidence is convincing, then presumably the agnostic would adopt the religion that provided the most compelling evidence of the interaction between realms. If the evidence is not convincing, then the agnostic would remain agnostic.

Note that an agnostic is not an atheist, but that an agnostic might

The Universal Life Church Ministries

convert to atheism in the same way that conversion to any other religion is possible: the agnostic would need to find convincing evidence supporting the adoption of that faith system.

Atheism

There are no universally known scientific tests for disproving the existence of spiritual things; therefore, atheism is a view based on a belief, unlike agnosticism which is arrived at empirically.

Atheists posit that gods or spirits do not exist. While some religions have atheistic elements to them (certain sects of Buddhism, for example), atheism itself is not a religion any more than bald is a hair color. Since there are neither a guiding scripture nor leader for atheism, the world views of atheists can differ wildly; the only common thread is the rejection of the supernatural.

Many people who are professed atheists are upset due to perceived injustices perpetuated by religious organizations. A common belief of atheists is that all known religions must be invalid by virtue of their causing mankind more harm than good. There are statistical tests for supporting this claim; however, such tests will never be conclusive and will always have a certain obvious degree of subjectivity in their interpretation.

Non-religion

Some people have a total lack of faith system, neither believing nor disbelieving in a spiritual realm but they are few and far between. The fact that these people are so rare is a matter of intense curiosity. There is strong evidence supporting the notion that there is something inherent in the human design which makes practically all people question whether or not a spiritual realm exists, if they doubt its existence at all.

"It appears to me (whether rightly or wrongly) that direct arguments against christianity [*sic*] and theism produce hardly any effect on the public; and freedom of thought is best promoted by the gradual illumination of men's minds which follows from the advance of science."
-*Darwin*

"If we believe absurdities, we shall commit atrocities."
-*Voltaire*

"I cannot imagine a God who rewards and punishes the objects of his creation, whose purposes are modeled after our own -- a God, in short, who is but a reflection of human frailty. Neither can I believe that the individual survives the death of his body, although feeble souls harbor such thoughts through fear or ridiculous egotism."
-*Einstein*

"Faith means not wanting to know what is true."
-*Nietzsche*

"I cannot believe in the immortality of the soul.... No, all this talk of an existence for us, as individuals, beyond the grave is wrong. It is born of our tenacity of life – our desire to go on living … our dread of coming to an end."
-*Edison*

"The Bible is not my book nor Christianity my profession. I could never give assent to the long, complicated statements of Christian dogma."
-*Lincoln*

"Religion is a by-product of fear. For much of human history, it may have been a necessary evil, but why was it more evil than necessary? Isn't killing people in the name of God a pretty good definition of insanity?"
-*Arthur C. Clarke*

"Religions are all alike – founded upon fables and mythologies."
-Thomas Jefferson

"Say what you will about the sweet miracle of unquestioning faith, I consider a capacity for it terrifying and absolutely vile."
-Kurt Vonnegut

"Religion is based . . . mainly on fear . . . fear of the mysterious, fear of defeat, fear of death. Fear is the parent of cruelty, and therefore it is no wonder if cruelty and religion have gone hand in hand. . . . My own view on religion is that of Lucretius. I regard it as a disease born of fear and as a source of untold misery to the human race."
- Bertrand Russell

Bahá'í Faith

Nine-pointed Star

> *"I bear witness, O my God, that Thou hast created me to know Thee and to worship Thee. I testify, at this moment, to my powerlessness and to Thy might, to my poverty and to Thy wealth. There is none other God but Thee, the Help in Peril, the Self-Subsisting."*
> - Bahá'u'lláh, Prayers and Meditations

Introduction

In 1844 CE a gentleman in Shiraz, Persia revealed that he was the Báb (gate) through whom a savior would become known to the world. In 1845 Bahá'u'lláh accepted the message of the Báb, fulfilled the prophesy in capacity as that savior, and founded the Bahá'í Faith as its prophet.

Bahá'u'lláh is the last in a series of great beings previously associated exclusively with particular religions, including Hinduism, Judaism, Zoroastrianism, Buddhism, Christianity, Islam, and many others.

Beliefs

Bahá'u'lláh's Kitáb-i-Aqdas (Most Holy Book), completed 1873, is the central book of the Bahá'í Faith. It is the basis for asserting the unity of Almighty God through the unity of all religious practices; in time, this connectedness of humankind through the Bahá'í Faith will bring peace, plenty, and fulfilment of all kinds to everyone on earth.

Customs

Bahá'ís must take to heart one of three obligatory prayers each day; the shortest one is quoted above. They observe the Bahá'í month of `Alá' from March 2 through March 20. Specific injunctions in their teachings meld their religious beliefs with the formality of civil law in matters of property ownership, marriage, and other

8

areas. Bahá'ís shun isolated living and enjoy participation in their social community, which if possible should include persons outside their religious community.

There is an expectation that Bahá'ís will seek righteousness and find the help of good counsel and good community to these ends.

Bahá'í Faith is not an Interfaith Religion

Bahá'í Faith is a religion which claims as ancestry most other great religions and prophets, but it is not an interfaith organization which will give full membership to adherents of non-Bahá'í faith. Bahá'ís respect the infallible authority of the Universal House of Justice, where an elected board of nine governs at its base in Haifa, Israel.

Certain personal characteristics which most people consider to be non-religious, such as choice to drink alcohol or the attribute of homosexuality, are specifically prohibited by a legacy of Bahá'í tradition in an effort to promote true righteousness over immediate or temporary worldly unity.

Bahá'í Faith is Compatible with Secular Facts

Bahá'í Faith promotes secular studies and promises doctrinal conformation with the discoveries of worldly authorities. To this end Bahá'í diplomats have a history of involvement with the United Nations (particularly the Economic and Social Council and the Children's Fund, or UNICEF), the World Health Organization, various international environmental protection agencies, and women's civil rights protectorates.

Bahá'í Faith encourages studies in physical sciences as well and took an early stand of support for new theories of all kinds prominent enough to be debated openly. While Bahá'í leaders often are silent about their personal views, the overall trend of the church is that fresh ideas are fairly assessed and, if appropriate, quickly assimilated into Bahá'í ideology.

Buddhism

I take refuge in the Buddha.
I take refuge in the doctrine.
I take refuge in the monastic order.
- Traditional and Liturgical

Introduction

Buddhism is probably the most simple religion describable, although it often is practiced with a modicum of cultural flair. Buddhism's chief tenets are called the Four Noble Truths, stated here:

1. Suffering exists.
2. Suffering has a cause, namely, desire.
3. Desire is the only cause of suffering.
4. There is a way to end desire.

That is the core of Buddhism; and one need only accept these statements to be a Buddhist. However, Buddhist practice also has specific traditions about applying these statements to real life. An elaboration on the fourth Noble Truth is the below Eightfold Path, which is a series of steps for Buddhist adherents to follow in order. Buddhists should attain these:

1. Right views
2. Right intention
3. Right speech
4. Right conduct
5. Right livelihood
6. Right strivings
7. Right mindset
8. Right concentration

The different ways in which the fourth Noble Truth is sought can define different religions. If one uses the Eightfold Path to

The Universal Life Church Ministries

attempt to achieve the fourth Noble Truth, then one uses Buddhist tradition.

History

The term "Buddha" comes from a Sanskrit word meaning "enlightened," "knowing," or "awake." In Buddhism it is used as a title for anyone who has achieved enlightenment.

The historical person called Buddha was Siddhartha Gautama, a prince born around 560 BCE in the northern part of the Indian subcontinent. His parents' wealth shielded him from all grief until his manhood, at which point he decided to explore places away from his luxurious upbringing.

For the first time in his life, he saw and learned of old age, disease, and death. He become horrified with the realization of the human condition, but then he saw an ascetic (monk) who was satisfied. He left his royal lifestyle and pursued the end to suffering; when he achieved this end, he taught the path he learned as the Buddha.

Spirituality

Buddhism as a faith tradition does not necessarily incorporate teachings about spirituality; however, various cultures often apply their own understandings about spirituality to Buddhism.

Some traditions teach that the aim of Buddhism is the actualization of nirvana, which is a form of enlightenment which is distinctly spiritual as well as earthly. Nirvana is neither nihilistic nor inclusive of all knowledge; it is a state associated with righteousness through moderation. Those who have achieved nirvana are free from samsara, or the cycle of death and rebirth.

Authority

Buddhism has no central authority but practitioners often adopt their culture's mores to interpret the faith.

The Dalai Lama, a Tibetan Buddhist, is an internationally renowned figurehead of the faith but not specifically a religious leader. He is only, in his own words, "a simple monk."

Cao Dai

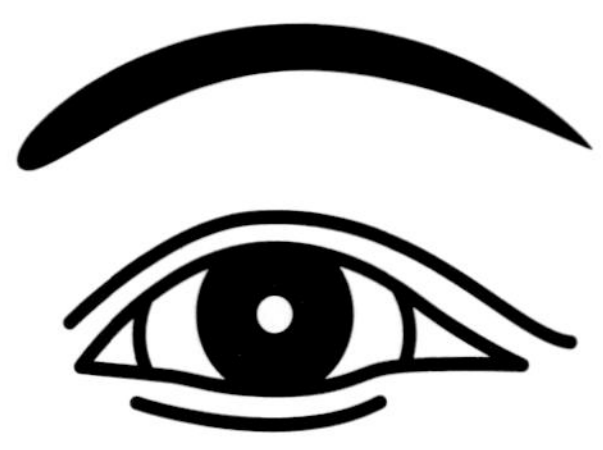

The Divine Eye

Introduction

Cao Dai, or, to give it its full title, Dai Dao Tam Ky Pho Do, is a religion that originated in South Vietnam in 1926. Dai Dao Tam Ky Pho Do translates into 'Great Religion of the Third Period of Revelation and Salvation' and adherents believe that the sect was created directly by God through his communication with its first four disciples. Cao Dai means 'Kingdom of Heaven' and the religion's ultimate goal is to free the believer from the repetitive cycle of birth and death.

History

The monotheistic Cao Dai saw the light of day in 1926 in the South Vietnamese city of Tay Ninh when, according to Caodaiist belief, God communicated directly with four followers and instructed them to establish a sect that would unite competing religious beliefs and assist people in joining God the Father in Heaven. Armed with, literally, heaven-sent information about the new religion's symbolism, teaching and hierarchical structure, the disciples established Cao Dai as an alternative to existing religions and as one which equally revered such usually mutually exclusive figures as Jesus Christ, the Buddha, Confucius and Laozi.

The initial four disciples were Cao Hoai Sang, Ngo Van Chieu, Pham Cong Tac and Cao Quynh Cu and, to date, they have been the people to have the greatest influence on the religion. Ngo Van Chieu later broke away from Cao Dai, however, and established the splinter sect called Chieu Minh, and at the same time refused appointment as the first Caodaiist Pope.

    The Universal Life Church Ministries

Today

Today Cao Dai has between 2.5 million and 8 million adherents in Vietnam, with a further 30,000 living in Australia, the USA and Europe. Although Cao Dai may be structured so that it's hierarchy resembles that of a democracy, the religion itself is anti-confrontational and does not involve itself in the politics of the countries in which its followers live.

Core Beliefs

In a nutshell, Caodaiists follow paths of nonviolence, prayer, the venetration of ancestors and vegetarianism so as to reach their goals of uniting with God and being released from the birth/death cycle. Followers are divided into three separate classes based upon which level they have reached in The Three Teachings, and these classes are, from lowest to highest, saint, sage and Buddha. Caodaiists also believe in gender equality - although women are not permitted to join the two highest Caodaiist religious ranks - and worship both God the Father as well as the Mother Buddha.

Christianity

Latin Cross

*I am the way, the truth, and the life. No one
comes to the Father except through Me.
- Jesus of Nazareth, Bible, Book of John 14:6*

Introduction

Christianity is a system of faith which promises infinite divine benefit to its adherents and possibly infinite divine punishment to its detractors. Its adherents are commonly understood to be those people who adopt a belief system defined by Almighty God and originally given to select members of mankind for the purposes of human dissemination and proselytization.

Founding

Jesus of Nazareth was born into a family of low economic class in approximately 1 CE, (his birth defined the modern dating system), in what is currently Palestine. The manner of His birth was unusual and fulfilled interpretations of Jewish prophecy in what Christians call the Old Testament. Before he reached adolescence he displayed unnatural wisdom beyond human education.

When Jesus was thirty years old He became an itinerant preacher and miracle worker. At this time He made statements which define the purpose of human existence. Also at this time Jesus of Nazareth revealed that He was, in fact, God incarnate as a man. As part of His purpose on earth Jesus submitted Himself to the human legal system and accepted a resulting governmental death penalty.

Salvation through Human Sacrifice

His death became the last instance of blood sacrifice in the Jewish tradition and is thought to atone for all possible sin, due to the infinite value of the divine human sacrifice. This fulfilled Jewish prophesy, as did His miraculous resurrection three days after His death.

The key concept in Christianity is that there is a protocol by means of which one may use that blood sacrifice to pay for personal failings which have offended God, who requires retribution in His capacity as ultimate judge. God has some just method for deciding a person's fate as a reincarnated spirit in the afterlife, and this decision is related to an individual's utilization of the blood sacrifice of Jesus.

Authority

Christianity has a closed canon of doctrine within an authoritative book created by God through men in generations after the advent of Jesus; this book is the New Testament which, together with the Old Testament, makes up a set of works called the Bible.

Christianity's largest authoritative body is the Holy See-- commonly regarded as either the Vatican or the Pope--which presides as head of the organization; fewer than half of all Christians recognize the authority of this body. Probably the most concise statement of Christianity is in the Nicene Creed or its derivatives; the sects of Christianity can generally be categorized by their reaction to this short document.

Missionary Tradition

Most of Christianity for most of history has held that those who die without accepting the doctrines of Christianity are doomed to Hell, a horrible fate in the afterlife. Because of this, many Christians insist that non-Christians be exposed to Biblical teachings. Some Christians consider the human-directed conversion of non-believers to Christianity to be more important than any other endeavor.

This belief is balanced in an informal way with the stronger notion that Almighty God is infinitely just, merciful, and loving; many believers find that they must reconcile that primary doctrine against all other doctrines, which are secondary.

Confucianism

Shui

*I transmit but do not create. I place my trust in
the teachings of antiquity.*
- Confucius, Analects VII

Introduction

Confucianism emphasizes harmony within human society, and to that end promotes a form of etiquette by means of which a civilization can achieve astounding and fulfilling spiritual and material greatness. This etiquette is the natural result of education, and by means of Confucianism one may learn of and practice right behavior with immediate benefit. Confucianism bears a strong resemblance to Western Secular Humanism; however, it has a legacy of academic excellence nearly unbroken for over two-thousand years.

Confucianism is a world religion embedded into Chinese folk religion and within Korean and Japanese social values. Since the twentieth century it has attracted converts in Europe and the United States without active solicitation.

Founding and Beliefs

Confucius was a great teacher born in China ca. 550 BCE. The major teachings of Confucius refer to a concept of li, which is a Chinese word meaning "offering" but which refers to formal ritual. Confucius loved li and used it as a means to inspire participants to profound accomplishments; at the same time, he sought to create the society which could appreciate, rather than simply perform, li. A related concept is that of ren, which is both a feeling of love for others and the attribute of benevolence. Within Confucianism, a person who is ren practices li. This lifestyle benefits society in measurable ways, while granting personal success and spiritual fulfilment to the practitioner.

The core value in Confucianism might be politeness. Whereas many other religions are introspective and private, Confucianism regards each person's active involvement in a community as being the means to fulfilment. Civility is a

The Universal Life Church Ministries

matter of respecting fundamental relationships, those being:

1. Child's obedience to parent's proper upbringing
2. Subject's good morality to ruler's benevolence
3. Wife's fidelity to husband's adoration
4. Young's respect to old's guidance
5. Friend's constancy to more-experienced friend's concern

In this hierarchy, the relationships are numbered in order of importance and listed so that the position on the left gives deference to the position on the right. Higher-ranking parties in the scheme are subject to ren criticism toward the goal of modeling the relationship after li.

These mutually beneficial relationships are permanent, even beyond death. In this way the relationships become part of a spiritual system of ancestor veneration, often improperly called "ancestor worship." Furthermore, the status of any position in this hierarchy is continually maintained by a system of merit. Such severance of interpersonal bonds is never done lightly; ren ideally leads to conflict resolution before problems arise.

Confucianism's open canon is standardized from these traditional texts:

1. Li Ji (Classic of Rites) - manual of Zhou court ceremony (Li); the model of procedure to achieve betterment in civilization
2. Yi-jing (I Ching, Classic of Changes) - yin-yang cosmological descriptions; comparable to environmentalism
3. Shu-jing (Classic of History) - data regarding Xia, Shang, and Zhou Dynasties; value of cultural tradition
4. Chun Qiu (Classic of Spring and Autumn) - a philosophical commentary on political events; applications of Li theory
5. Shi-jing (Classic of Poetry) - Zhou Dynasty poetry with cultural significance; egalitarian spirituality of all mankind

Cosmology

Confucianist social theory offers immediate benefits to all practitioners, regardless of spiritual beliefs, but the philosophy might be best grounded in religion as Confucius himself taught it should be. Li ultimately results in betterment to participants, so although it might mention Tian (heaven), all of the benefit comes from its actual execution and not from a divine response to li. The Yi-jing (I Ching) elaborates on spiritual concepts of a force called qi; Confucianism sees more physical explanations for benefits from qi than a related religion, Taoism.

Hinduism

Om

For certain is death for the born, and certain is birth for the dead, therefore over the inevitable, thou shouldst not grieve.
- Bhagavad Gita, Chapter 2 Verse 27

Introduction

Hinduism is the term used to describe a vast collection of loosely-related faith practices native to the Indian subcontinent. The practices described below are popular but not definitive or even inclusive of most Hindus.

Recurrent Concepts throughout Hinduism

There is something sacred or blessed about the very geography of the Indian subcontinent.

There might ultimately be one Almighty God. He has three most powerful forms: that of Brahman, the Creator of All; Shiva, Destroyer of All; and Vishnu, Preserver of All. This Almighty God also takes other forms, and popularly the forms are numbered as 330 million, and many forms act as individual deities. Some Hindus say that there are many gods and yet only an Almighty God; or some just say there are many gods and say nothing of an Almighty God. This is a difficult concept for non-Hindus but sensible to Hindus.

After death one's soul (spiritual essence) leaves one's body and migrates into a new body. This is called samsara (reincarnation).

The design of the universe contains an inherent and personal dharma (duty) for each creature; it is beneficial to recognize and accept this duty. Dharma changes in every incarnation of a soul.

The design of the universe contains an inherent system of applying merit based on a creature's adherence to its dharma; this system is called karma. Karma stays the same as a soul reincarnates.

There is a form of enlightenment by which one can escape

The Universal Life Church Ministries

samsara and join Vishnu. This enlightenment involves recognizing maya (illusion) and thereby achieving moksha (enlightenment).

Vishnu loves humanity and wants humanity to seek Him. He incarnates Himself on earth periodically when righteousness declines and unrighteousness increases; while on earth he then augments the former and combats the latter.

Three of Vishnu's latest forms have been Rama (born 7400 BCE), a dutiful warrior whose story is contained in the epic Ramayana; Krishna (born 3200 BCE), an intensely physically and mentally attractive cowherd and prince whose story is told in the epic Mahabharata; and Buddha (born 560 BCE), founder of Buddhism.

There is an associated concept of caste relating to Dharma; this concept may or may not have been radically altered by British occupation. Strictly speaking, only Hindus have caste, but in social practice, many classes of society from all religions exhibit intercaste formality.

India's Peaceful Residents

Hindu tradition has been the formative background for the nurturing of other religions, notably Zoroastrianism (through Parsis), Buddhism, Sikhism, and Jainism. Historically, these faith systems and Hinduism itself have produced some of the highest philosophical treatises on the topic of peaceful living.

None of these other religions have any basis in Hinduism; they were founded separately from Hindu religious influence.

Conclusion

It is not the case that one form or teaching of Vishnu is most important; it is one's dharma which directs one to glorify Almighty God in the appropriate way. However, Rama and Krishna are wildly popular.

Humanism

Humanism Icon

Introduction

Humanism is a tradition of values that emphasizes the importance of human dignity, virtue, capabilities, and concerns. It does not directly consider the question of the existence of God, but rather the morality and ethics of human conduct; for humanists, the morality of the individual's conduct remains a crucial consideration whether or not a god exists, hence there are both theist and atheist humanists. Of the ethics which undergird humanist philosophy, rationality is strongly emphasized: those who follow this philosophy strive to base all of their convictions, religious or secular, on sound evidence and reasoning.

History

The birth of humanism can be traced as far back as 1000 BCE to the Lokayata philosophy of India. Around the sixth century BCE, Taoist teacher Laozi imported this philosophy to China, where Confucius was also teachings ethics which centered on human conduct. In the Pali texts of the Buddhist tradition, Gautama Buddha showed skepticism about the supernatural world, arguing that it is absurd to believe that human existence is permanent if neither a soul nor anything associated with it exists.

Also in the sixth century BCE, humanistic philosophy arose in the Ionian Greek world with the pantheists Thales of Miletus and Xenophanes of Colophon. While Xenophanes rejected the gods of his time and recognized the principle of unity with the universe, Thales is credited with the maxim, "Know thyself". Other classical

The Universal Life Church Ministries

Greek humanists who relied on reason and criticized superstition include Anaxagoras, reputedly the first "free thinker", his pupil, Pericles, Democritus and Protagoras, and Thucydides. Epicurus, the first Greek philosopher to admit women into his schools, challenged belief in the afterlife while also tackling the problem of evil, showing the ability of the philosopher to consider moral questions apart from the supernatural.

Humanism re-emerged in the late Middle ages and Renaissance as an intellectual movement in western Europe. The Italian poet Petrarch was possibly the first pre-modern humanist and was the first to identify a definite "dark age" between the fall of the western Roman Empire in 476 and his own time. As a solution to medieval "ignorance", Petrarch suggested the study of classical liberal arts, such as rhetoric, poetry, and grammar, by figures such as Cicero. Many scholars agree that these medieval *umanistas* were not secular humanists in the modern sense, but were often involved in the church and were sometimes even priests.

The modern understanding of humanism—especially secular humanism—originated largely with the French Enlightenment: a French periodical of 1765 defined the term as a "love of humanity". Enlightenment thinkers adopted this sense of humanism to extol the virtues of the human being irrespective of the supernatural. This emerging secular humanism was attacked by religious and political conservatives who opposed the French Revolution and the philosophy of Enlightenment thinkers such as Rousseau, and secular humanists have struggled ever since to portray their belief system in a positive light.

Beliefs

Religious humanists believe in sufficient evidence for the existence of God, but they do not accept claims of Biblical inerrancy, while secular humanists generally find insufficient evidence for the existence of God, and hence many of them are atheists or agnostics. In addition, humanists emphasize the importance of life in the present world rather than in an afterlife. Of itself, atheism has nothing to say about morality or life purpose—it is simply the doctrine that there is no God. Since atheism concerns itself with the existence of God, and not necessarily human virtues, humanism takes up where atheism leaves off by shifting the focus back on these virtues. In their effort to realize humanity's full potential, modern humanists often endorse scientific skepticism and the scientific method. Social justice issues are central concerns for all humanists; among these issues are gender and racial equality, reproductive rights, civil rights, freedom of and from religion, and separation of church and state.

Humanism has no sacred text which codifies humanist beliefs. However, the writings of many humanists over thousands of years comprise an informal, evolving canon. Important early figures in humanism were Socrates, Aristotle and Confucius, all of whose works were seminal in the development of the philosophy. Among the most important modern humanist philosophers have been Brand Blanshard, a professor of philosophy at Yale University, and Thomas Hurka, a professor of philosophy at the University of Calgary. In general, humanists place a great deal of emphasis on living a full life, with a rich variety of experiences and accomplishments, and in contributing to the quality of life of others as well. Those who try to make the world a better place are living humanistically.

Humanists do not believe in self-realization at the cost of "weeding out the weak". The phrase "survival of the fittest" is derived from the theory of evolution originally proposed by Charles Darwin. They do believe that human beings, like every other living thing, evolved from simpler organisms, but they believe that the evolutionary process itself does not provide an ethical standard. Like many religions, humanism endorses the golden rule: "Do unto others as you would have them do unto you."

Humanism and Religion

The attitudes of humanists towards the world's religions vary widely. Some humanists, having been persecuted for their convictions, or seeing religion as superstitious, have an active dislike of all forms of religion; others recognize value in religion, though in a very questioning, seeking way; others yet are somewhere in between, seeing religion as a mixed blessing which consists of both oppressive or irrational dogma as well as universal human principles.

Many humanists believe there is great need of religious reform and enlightenment. While advances in science and technology have been highly profitable, and thus practical to invest in, philosophy has generated few, if any, fortunes, and has therefore had few benefactors in the business sector. The consequence, from a humanist perspective, is that we have become spiritual barbarians in possession of tremendously powerful weapons and tools. Hence, humanists see a need to return to a state of self-reflection.

Although it has been argued that God is necessary to define morality, history has shown otherwise. The Japanese, for example, developed an ethic known as Bushido which was non-spiritual but nevertheless served as a code of conduct; although a mixed blessing, it was at least no more destructive than organized religion. Similarly, the Chinese philosophy of Confucianism has served as a non-spiritual code of ethics for the Chinese, largely with beneficial effects. Just like everybody else, these humanists have shown moral lapses due to the fallibility of human nature; nevertheless, both of these non-religious doctrines served large numbers of people well for long periods of time.

Critics of humanism might wonder how humanists can think of life as meaningful without considering the existence of God. However, many humanists would point out that life is meaningful because of good relationships, fulfilling work, and so on, and that these things are valuable whether or not there is a God to make determine their value. For humanists, God would commend these things because they are intrinsically valuable, and not just because God exists to deem them so.

Islam

*There is no god but Allah (Almighty God) and
Muhammad is His prophet.
- Shahada (Creed of Islam)*

Ottoman Empire Mark

<u>Introduction</u>

Islam is a religion which traces its founding to an agreement which Allah (Almighty God) had with Ibrahim, (Abraham), in 2000 BCE. Since then, Allah established a final covenant through a final prophet Muhammad, born 570 CE. This covenant involves respect for Allah's instructions contained verbatim in the Qur'an as given to Muhammad; in return Allah promises infinite reward in Jannah (a paradise garden) after death. Most Muslims believe that Allah will punish in a finite way those who did not accept the covenant in this life, after which comes the possibility of entering Jannah.

<u>Practices</u>

Muslims have in common five practices, known as the Five Pillars of Islam. These are the following:

1. Recitation of the Shahadah, as written above
2. Salat, or prayer five times daily
3. Zakat, or the giving of alms toward
    charitable world-betterment
4. Sawn, or fasting during the holy month of Ramadan
5. Hajj, or the pilgrimage to Mecca in Saudi Arabia

The consensus is that each of these practices is beneficial to oneself and to one's community, and therefore pleasing to Allah. Also note that each one of these practices is intimately connected with education, as the Shahadah and salat must be backed with understanding; the zakat must be used in a maximally economical way; the Ramadan is a time for study; and the Hajj is an intellectual as well as spiritual learning adventure.

Importance of Messenger and Location

All Muslims believe that Muhammad presented the Qur'an to the world in a perfect way; the majority of people would not otherwise argue that Muhammad was divine. Most people believe that Allah chose Muhammad to bear the Qu'ran, and other than that, he was simply a righteous man like other prophets.

Mecca is a city of historical significance to Muslims and it is prominent as a place from which Allah chose to deliver his message to mankind. In Mecca there is al-Masjid al-Haram (The Sacred Mosque) which contains the Kaaba. Ibrahim and his firstborn son, Ismail, built the Kaaba with explicit instructions from Allah. It is the holiest site in Islam, and Muslims face the Kaaba when praying.

Spirituality

Islam is legalistic, as is its historical tradition from People of the Book (Jews and Christians). The major sects tend to integrate beliefs formally into the laws of society and sometimes seem to view Allah as a director of worldly affairs through human devotees rather than as a personally intervening entity.

There are other, more mystical, sects of Islam, notably Sufism, the followers of which seek to experience Allah in a direct way through spiritual communion.

Authority

Islam has no central authority. While Christianity and Judaism – the previous Abrahamic traditions - also claim to have unadulterated Word of God, Islamic belief is much stricter about propagation of the Word in that the Qu'ran is untranslatable from the original Arabic. All attempts to publish the Qu'ran in other languages are flawed, and therefore its interpretation solely as an Arabic text is more evident and requires less commentary.

Jainism

Jain Hand

Introduction

Jainism is an ancient religion from India promoting non-violence, for all beings in the universe, as the only acceptable means of experiencing life. Basically, it's a constant attempt for the soul ascending onward to reach an apex of spirituality. When a soul has reached Jina, the most enlightened state, it means that all of the inner demons have been exorcised, and an inner equilibrium is reached.

Spirituality

Some of the major spiritual points of Jainism are the following: every living creature has a soul; every soul can potentially become divine through knowledge, harmony, and power. Every being should be treated with equal respect, this means hurting no one. Each entity or soul is born human, sub-human, hellish, or celestial, as far as karma is concerned. Each being is the creator of his or her life, in this one or hereafter. The moment a soul has relinquished its karma, only then can divine consciousness, knowledge, infinite perception, and peace become a reality. Jainism focuses a lot on mastering the senses, as they have proven to lead the individual into vice—further from the spiritual self. In addition, owning physical objects and wealth are okay, so long as unhealthy attachment does not take place. By removing one's self of negative, unenlightened thoughts through what is referred to as clearance or karmic repair, the individual ascends into the divine nature and aligns his or herself with the most enlightened spirits.

The Universal Life Church Ministries

<u>Practices</u>

Some of the current practices regarding Jainism have to do with participating is asceticism. This idea typically refers to minimizing one's indulgences, and taking on habits of maintaining one's health through diet, no matter how difficult it becomes. Being a vegetarian is essential, for otherwise it would be aggressive towards animals, which is obviously against their beliefs. Another important aspect of Jainism has to do with stopping the cycle of transmigration, namely ending one's ill ways in this life, so that there won't be another one afterwards. Hopefully, at the end of the life, the individual will not need to repeat it because the karmic business has been finished. On a daily basis, a typical Jain worship is a universal prayer, "Namokara Mantra," and includes symbols offered as reminder of their path to attain the revered Moksha, or the ultimate liberation.

Juche

North Korea

Overview

Juche is the official ideology of North Korea. The word Juche is translated to "self-reliance" in the Korean language. The religion was originally created by Kim Il-sung, a Korean communist politician, in 1956. Juche was originally more of a political ideology than a religious one. However, during the early 1960s, Juche transformed into a much more spiritual ideology.

Kim Il-sung defined Juche as "the independent stance of rejecting dependence on others and of using one's own powers, believing in one's own strength and displaying the revolutionary spirit of self-reliance." Outsiders often define the ideology as a mandatory philosophy that calls for loyalty to the communist party.

Beliefs / Principles

In 1965, Kim Il-sung outlined three fundamental principles of Juche: chaju, or independence in politics; charip (self-sustenance in the economy) and chawi, or self-defense in national defense. Subsequent leaders of North Korea, also recognize Juche as the official ideology of the nation, and have declared themselves each the main and final authority on all matters concerning the Juche Idea.

Criticism

Today, it is widely debated as to whether or not Juche can truly be denied as a religion. Many people argue that Juche fits into the category of religion, as it has millions of extremely devoted followers. Sociologists argue that Juche is indeed a religion, and more of a religion than either Chinese Maoism or Soviet communism. According to Thomas Belke, author of "JUCHE: A Christian Study of North Korea's State Religion", Juche is clearly a religion, with "more adherents than Judaism, Sikhism, Jainism or Zoroastrianism." Those who believe Juche is a religion also point to the fact that Juche has adopted several of the ideas promoted by Confucius. In addition, there are a number of "ceremonies" conducted in the name of Juche, as well as what outsiders often label "holy sites."

Still, promoters of Juche define it as a secular philosophy rather than a religion in the traditional sense. They often point to the fact that it was created by Kim Il-sung as a means of staying out of the conflict between Soviet Russia and Communist China, not as a result of a near death experience or an experience involving some sort of "God" or God-like figure. Also, followers of Juche claim to be atheists and as such, feel that following Juche can in no way be religious.

Whether or not Juche is truly a religion, with millions of followers, it certainly has an impact on today's world!

Judaism

What is hateful to you do not do to your neighbor. That is the whole Torah - the rest is commentary.
- Talmud, Tractate Shabbat 31A

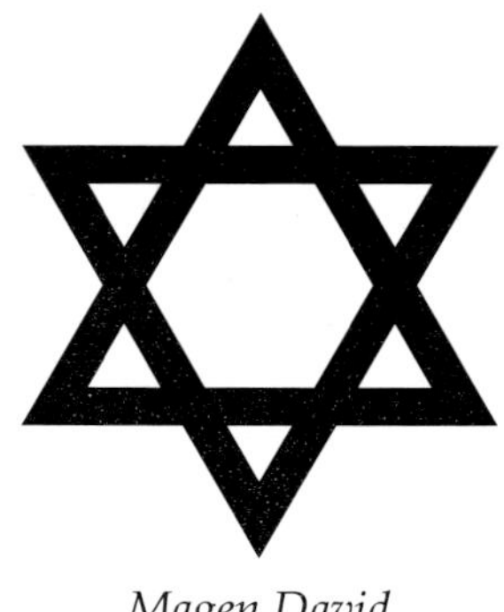

Magen David

Introduction

The word "Jewish" denotes a culture, a religion, and also a set of ethnicities which cross numerous races, times, and geographical areas; therefore, being a Jew can mean adhering to certain customs for either social or spiritual reasons, or in other cases it merely denotes that a person is of a certain parentage.

The traditional Jewish religion, Judaism, likewise is cross-cultural in that those who have no ethnic ties to the religion may yet respectfully practice it. The faith system of Judaism states that various prominent Jews in history entered contractual relationships with Almighty God on behalf of the Jewish people; the agreements tend toward God asking the Jews to do something natural and wholesome. In return God bestows an abundance of sublime favor onto the Jewish people.

Jewish Books and Authority

The authority of Judaism is vested in writings and traditions and not in any governing body. The Hebrew Bible consists of these three books: the Torah, or the Five Books of Moses; the Nevi'im, or the Prophets; and the Ketuvim, or the Writings. The Torah has prime influence over these, but this collection of texts has been preserved continuously for many thousands of years.

Judaism is a religion with a closed canon but retains exceptional respect for other books. The Talmud is a set of commentaries completed around 400 CE by rabbis (Jewish teachers) who have interpreted the Torah. Scholars of Jewish mysticism recorded their

The Universal Life Church Ministries

observations into the Kabbalah; the Zohar (Book of Splendor) is a contained text which expounds ten created Sephiroth (enumerations) by means of which God created the universe. The Haggadah is a detailed retelling of the Exodus from Egypt and is widely embedded into Hebrew tradition.

Jewish History

Judaism was founded around 2000 BCE in the region which is now termed the Middle East through a man named Abraham, who was a member of a nomadic tribe called the Hebrews, who later were called the Israelites.

There is a dynasty of God-fearing men chronicled in the Torah. The history goes as such: A man named Noah built a boat upon command by God. God flooded the earth, sparing only Noah and his family. One of Noah's sons, Shem, was the ancestor of Abraham. God spoke to Abraham, saying "I will make you a great nation." Abraham's successor Jacob founded the Jewish nation of Israel.

Abraham's descendents figure prominently in Jewish history, but also in fulfillment of that Jewish prophesy both Jesus of Nazareth, founder of Christianity, and Muhammad, who established Islam, claim lineage back to Abraham. Discussion of the significance of this prophesy is often emotionally reactive to Jews, Christians, and Muslims.

Jewish Spirituality

Jewish people share a history as a nation in exile and attach great value to their State of Israel, restored in 1947. While many Jews are secular, practically all take pride from at least some aspects of their culture's history and efficiency.

Jews put emphasis on successful living. Although many Jews believe in an afterlife, most authorities say that preparing for it is either futile or simply best done by living a meaningful human existence.

Natural Law

Scale of Balance

Introduction

Natural Law is the concept that life forms have a certain function and purpose. When beings live according to their scientifically evident purpose then nature generates benefit; when life is artificially forced into non-functional, illogical roles then nature generates problems.

Beliefs

Natural Law asserts that humankind has inherent in its very design, as evidenced by its very existence, certain inalienable and God-given rights. These rights can be readily determined by assessment of actions for harm and benefit; if a certain action is beneficial to a person, and if that action causes no harm to others, then execution of that action should be an inherent right associated with human existence.

Natural Law is also the name given to the social and religious movements which spontaneously arise in civilizations of all eras when a minority group faces oppression from a society which enacts decisions against natural law.

Practitioners of natural law believe prejudice is a social ill which resurfaces, causing strife in all ages. It must be recognized to be understood and fairly judged to be extinguished, leaving merit and the inherent value of the soul as the measure of human worth.

History

Persons citing Natural Law as a cause for social change have typically done so with an abundance of scientific backing, but at the risk of societal backlash. Victories over societal and religious injustice include the repeal of discrimination based on gender, creed, class, caste, age, race, skin color, and sexual orientation.

During the 1940s, Germany's fascist Nazi political regime rounded up millions of people who were members of groups which, by Natural Law, had a right to liberty. Alleged homosexuals comprised one of these groups; all gays were labeled with a pink triangle sewn onto their prison clothes as the first step on a planned route of extermination. In response to this atrocity, gays have reclaimed the pink triangle as a symbol of pride and willingness to fight back whenever oppression rears its head again. Interestingly, both the Christian cross and pink triangle are former symbols of execution.

Natural law has also confronted religious oppression of minority groups. Columbia University Biblical scholar Morton Smith claims that in 1958, at the Mar Saba Monastery near Jerusalem, he found a fragment of a letter from Clement, Bishop of Alexandria, to Theodore, the priest of an early Christian community. The letter includes a suppressed passage which was omitted from the text of St. Mark, chapter 10 (between verses 34 and 35 in the standard version of the Bible). The passage, dated ca. 95 CE, relates how Jesus went with a wealthy youth to the latter's house; after staying six days, Jesus "instructed" the boy, who came to Jesus later that evening, scantily clad, at which point Jesus "taught him the mystery of the Kingdom of God."

In an attempt to expose this suppression, human rights activist Peter Tatchell argues there is scant information on Jesus's sexuality: "Since there is no proof of the heterosexuality of Jesus, the theological basis of Church homophobia is all the more shaky and indefensible." According to Tatchell, the "Church sanitized the gospels, removing references to Christ's sexuality that were not in accord with the heterosexual morality that it wanted to promote".

Neopaganism

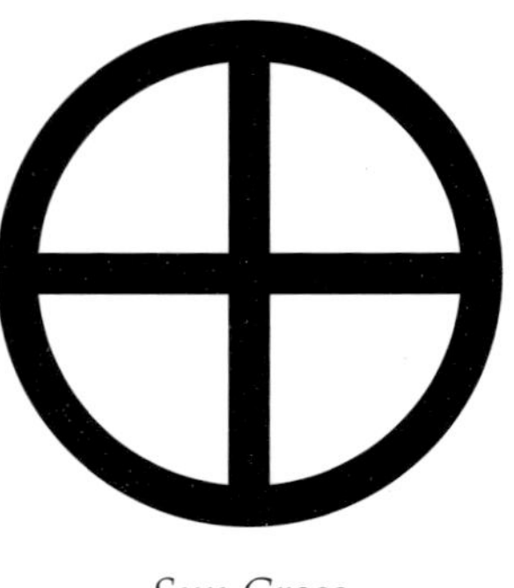

Sun Cross

As it harms none, do as thou wilt.
- Traditional, from Crowley and Wiccan Rede

Introduction

Neopaganism is a revivalist movement powered by an amalgamation of primal traditions from various geographical areas and eras. An uncodified faith system with no central authority, it does not have many adherents or a set of canonical faith texts; and it is exemplified by almost personal faith practices and extreme variation in belief, purpose, and custom. One concept that has gained wide acceptance in Neopaganist thought is that each person should do what they decide is 'right,' with the term being defined as what benefits themselves and causes harm to no other.

Diversity

"Neopagan" refers to a reclamation of the formerly pejorative term "pagan," used by Abrahamic religious tradition to refer to primal traditional faith practices everywhere in the world. While the original primal religions were localized and even sometimes exclusive to their adherents, the neopagan movement has adopted a policy of universal acceptance and wide assimilation of the practices of many cultures. Common characteristics of all branches of neopaganism include reverence for surroundings--usually natural, but sometimes urban--and the ability to personally direct material world change through the control of spiritual forces.

One of the most popular and best-established branches of neopaganism is Wicca, which is a system incorporating magic and which may venerate a Goddess, Horned God, or other deities. Wicca itself is sectarian, almost to the point where most neopagans fit someone's definition of "Wicca."

Other popular branches of Neopaganism include types of

The Universal Life Church Ministries

animism; specifically Shamanism, which is typically a leadership-based and intuitive system of spiritual interaction; and Druidism, which is typically a communally-led and ritualistic system of spiritual interaction. Neopaganism has enacted the rise of scientifically-integrated physical, mental, and spiritual healing practice systems involving techniques such as ayurveda, yoga, acupuncture, massage, herbalism, alchemy, and psychonautical travel.

Newness and Lack of Educational Resources

Unfortunately, the demand for spiritual fulfillment in the Neopagan faith system is currently in crisis as many who are interested in Neopaganism are at a loss to find good teachers, be those teachers practicing Neopagans or simply good books due to the lack of history and ritualistic tradition. Undoubtedly Neopaganism will grow in value and importance over time.

Necessity of Community

Neopaganism is currently difficult to explain in text form due to its rich varieties of practices. Interested parties are encouraged to join a Neopagan community to get guidance from a practicing and experienced Neopagan or even start a new Neopagan community, rather than attempt solitary research in books.

The Internet can be key resources for finding other Neopagans. Neopagans tend to congregate in cities in spite of the preference to perform rituals in a natural setting. To remedy to this problem is a community issue much like successful churches of older faiths incorporate social networks to serve their members' needs.

Organizations

The New Age movement is currently dispersed in the sense that no one organization has made enough of a significant contribution to achieve wide renown. Almost all successful New Age practitioners are talented individuals associated with either small schools or churches, private research firms, or simply their own family or community.

New Age

Intelligence may control the mechanism of civilization, wisdom may direct it, but spiritual idealism is the energy which really uplifts and advances human culture from one level of attainment to another.
- Urantia Book, 81:6 (page 909)

Lemniscate or Infinity

Introduction

New Age refers to a movement through which spirituality comes under investigation by science with positive findings. Science can be defined as the compilation of subjective real-world events into objective numerical data for the purpose of interpreting past events and with the hope of predicting future events. Traditional sciences, which stem from physics, measure things in the material realm. The New Age movement is intimately associated with a branch of science called "metaphysics," which deals with the first principles of things, particularly abstract concepts such as substance, space, identity, and time. As such, it has become colloquially synonymous with the study of the spiritual realm.

Legacy of Research

New Age does not yet have a canon and instead has preserved its tradition over the centuries with continual rewriting of concepts to better benefit different time periods. The texts that would potentially be in the canon, such as the Confucian Yi-jing (called I Ching or Classic of Changes), the ancient Egyptian mathematical theory from the Book of the Dead, Jewish Kabbalah's Zohar, Hindu Vedanta practices from the Upanishads, and other applications of scientific method to spirituality are currently studied in concentrated geographical areas. There is a major concern in that much of the knowledge of primal traditions – sometimes called "pagan" – is not currently accessible through books or the Internet.

                                   The Universal Life Church Ministries

Organizations

The New Age movement is currently dispersed in the sense that no one organization has made enough of a significant contribution to achieve wide renown. Almost all successful New Age practitioners are talented individuals associated with either small schools or churches, private research firms, or simply their own family or community.

Spirituality

A common teaching within New Age faith is that all beings have a spiritual essence. This essence may either be personal to an individual – as in notions of Ancient Egyptian ba, Hindu atman, or the soul of Abrahamic traditions - or it may be an actual fragment of the Creator's infinite spiritual essence – as in the notion of Buddha-nature.

There is extreme variation of teaching otherwise, but the care of spiritual needs often is as much of a priority as intellectual or bodily interests.

Extraterrestrial Life

Some practitioners within the New Age movement believe in the material form of the Creator's most devoted celestial servants; this is in contrast to most other faith traditions which hold that beings such as angels or devas are primarily spiritual entities.

Successful Practice

Those who benefit from New Age are typically those who best balance intuition with science. Science demands that all practices follow a method; generally, if a given practice can be taught, learned, or transferred from one person to another, then it is methodical and therefore metaphysical. If a given practice is unique to an individual then it probably is not metaphysical, and might better be classified as spiritual in some other sense.

Primal Faith

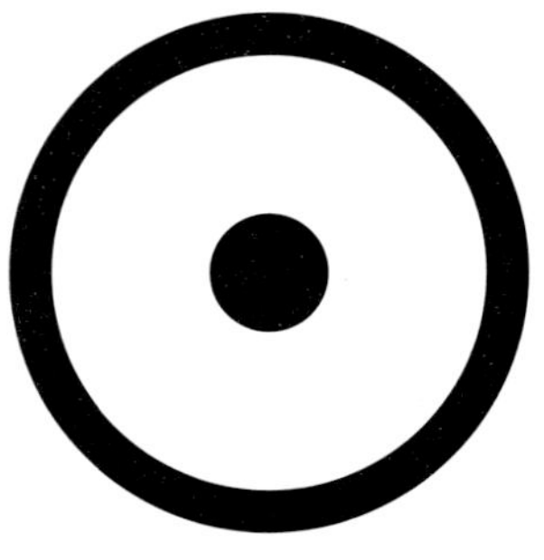

Free choice and opportunity, not race, creed, gender, orientation, caste, class, or color make people different.
- Universal Life Church Monastery Mission

Introduction

Some religions are primal faith traditions, meaning that they existed at the beginning of recorded history. Few of these exist as major world religions today; however as examples, certain beliefs in Hinduism, Chinese folk religion, Zoroastrianism, and Judaism probably qualify to be called "primal."

Most primal traditions were localized and did not have missionary conversion doctrines. Over time, a paradigm emphasizing proselytism dominated world politics and certain religions became prominent as other religions went into decline or total non-practice. Of the three world religions with a tradition of converting non-believers to their belief systems – Buddhism, Christianity, and Islam – the latter two have been particularly domineering worldwide in the forcefulness of their propagation. Christians usually referred to primal faith traditions as "pagan," while Muslims usually referred to them as what is translated to mean "idolators." Both of these terms are derogatory within those religions.

There typically is no connection between any one primal faith tradition and another. Even primal traditions in close geographical proximity or in different groups within a cultural or ethic category can vary to the point of complete differentiation. The fact that primal faith traditions are grouped together in this book is due to an ability to give fair treatment to any of them.

A goal of this book is to be concise and meaningful to the greatest number of readers. An overview of each is not possible within that goal. Interested parties should do their own research and be aware that many primal faith traditions are preserving their doctrines by means of Internet documentation and awareness campaigns.

　　　　　The Universal Life Church Ministries

Primal Faith Traditions by Geography

Africa is a continent which contains areas subjected to wide-scale human rights abuses of the worst kinds for at least centuries. Through no fault of their own, indigenous peoples there have had their faiths shaken in literally ungodly ways. Those that remain are soulful, steadfast, inspirational, and in need of increased global awareness without further shocking intervention.

Most European native traditions are chronicled in history as being converts. Some traditions are well-documented otherwise; some exist even today.

Northern Siberia's native traditions remained intact longer than elsewhere in Russian Federation due to that land being less economically desirable than other places in modern times. Heavily populated places became homogeneous more readily.

When the "New World" was "discovered" by Westerners in the late fifteenth century CE, it was actually already inhabited in most viable regions. Very few indigenous peoples north of Mexico live without thorough integration into non-indigenous society. Often the decimation of native religion in the Americas is paired with decimation of native renewable resources.

Likewise, when Australia was "discovered" in the early seventeenth century CE, Aborigines and the Torres Strait Islanders had already settled the land and established a shared spirituality. The debate about the impact of this "discovery" is known in Australia as the "History Wars."

Pacific Island tribal faiths are some of the best preserved still in practice.

China has been recovering from an identity crisis stemming from the British Opium Wars in the early nineteenth century; since then its government has taken varying stands on the status of native religion.

India has legal protections in place since the mid-twentieth century for what are called "Scheduled Tribes," "Scheduled Castes," and "Other Backward Classes."

Middle Eastern native traditions were documented in various ways. A great tragedy of the twenty-first century was the public loss of Mesopotamian religious artifacts in the American / Iraqi War.

Primal Indigenous

The Big Bang

Introduction

Primal indigenous religion, although not a single, organized religion, accounts for the belief systems of 300 million people in Africa and Asia. These religions are the outcome of traditional, native world views and infiltrate every aspect of the lives of whom they are practiced.

Due to variations in tradition, region, and ethnicity, there are many surface differences between the diverse primal religions, though they share basic overlying concepts. Anthropologists and academics have previously compared primal religions to paganism, shamanism, and animism, and while they do share similarities, these comparisons have largely been abandoned.

Spirituality

Followers of primal indigenous religions are henotheistic, that is, they worship one god while acknowledging the existence of others. God dwells within all things and all things are spiritual in nature. All of existence is thought to be connected, including life and death, humans and animals, the physical world and spirit world, etc.

As mentioned, primal religions do not discern between the physical and the spiritual, nor is there a hard distinction between worship and other day-to-day activities of life. Living in and of itself is a spiritual act - the duties of each day are so intertwined with nature and the earth that they are regarded as spiritual, as opposed to compartmentalizing life in to "work", "leisure", and "worship". The primal concept of time is also different - time is not linear as western cultures think of it and instead the idea of "timelessness" is accepted. Rituals are enacted as performances of the original act and are ever-present and thus link individuals to the eternity through the present.

Demographics & Rituals

Cultures who practice tribal indigenous religions are generally pre-literate and lack written language. Their beliefs and traditions are orally disseminated, usually through stories. These stories are passed down through the generations to explain the origin of man, nature of God, and explanations of the world's workings. Often these stories are tied to the region in which they are told, as followers are closely tied to the earth and the locale in which they live.

Rites of passage are of great importance in these societies, as is the concept of liminality, the state of transition between various rites of passage. Rites of passage are distinguished by rituals, which play a large role in tribal life. The tribe, which extends beyond just persons and includes nature, animals, and objects both animate and inanimate, is central to the individual's sense of self.

Rastafarianism

Lion of Judah

Introduction

Rastafarianism is a modern religious movement that has arisen from the tenets of Judaism and Christianity. Also known as the Rastafari movement, Rastafarianism is not a traditional highly organized religion, like it's ancestors, Judaism and Christianity. Some Rastas (adherents of Rastafarianism) seek to dispose completely of the notion that Rastafarianism is a religion at all. These Rastas prefer to think of Rastafarianism as a "way of life."

Spirituality & Beliefs

Rastafarianism is a monotheistic religion. The Rastas refer to this God as "Jah" and, similar to Christianity, see Jah in the form of the Holy Trinity (Father, Son and Holy Ghost). Rastas emphasize that in the Holy Ghost form, Jah can be found within all human beings. Rastas also agree with Christians that Jesus Christ is God incarnate. They believe, however, that the teachings and legacy of Jesus Christ were corrupted by Western Society, which they often refer to as "Babylon." They believe that Jesus was black, and that he is only depicted as white as a result of the West's corruption of Christianity.

The Rastas claim that Africa (and especially Ethiopia) has been promised to them by Jesus Christ. They refer to these Holy lands as Zion. They also believe that they are the real Children of Israel. This belief can be seen in the strong Afrocentrism evident in Rastafarianism. Also present in Rastafarianism is the concept of "Black Pride." Many early Rastas believed in the idea of black

The Universal Life Church Ministries

supremacy, but later, Rastafarianism evolved to accept people of any ethnicity, as they came to believe that the religion should belong to all humans.

Scripture & Ceremony

Being an Abrahamic religion, Rastafarianism draws heavily from the Bible. The New Testament Book of Revelation is considered the most important piece of scripture. Many adherents of Rastafarianism believe that the written Bible makes up only half of the true Bible. These Rastas believe that the other half of the Bible can be found in one's own heart.

There are two major ceremonies that members of Rastafarianism engage in. One ceremony is called reasoning, and consists of a gathering of Rastas who smoke cannabis and discuss political, philosophical and ethical issues of the day. Groundation, the other major ceremony of Rastafarianism is a holy day during which Rastas sing, dance, smoke cannabis and recite a prayer very similar to the Christian Lord's Prayer.

Shinto

*The heart of the person before you is a mirror. See
there your own form.
- Traditional Shinto maxim*

Torii

Introduction

Shinto is the religion culturally and geographically tied to
Japan. Its practice of acknowledging kami (spirits) dates to at least
100 BCE, which coincides with Japan's founding as a state.

Shinto practices are animistic, meaning they recognize that kami
reside in living and non-living things, and they are shamanistic,
meaning that Shinto adherents are able to utilize the kami nature of
things in controllable and useful ways. Typically, Shinto is used to
purify people, places, and things of troublesome spiritual pollution.
Shinto ceremonies themselves are often exceedingly formal by
the standards of many other religions; however, this formality is
an entirely pleasurable experience within the context of Japanese
culture.

Customs and Beliefs

Kami are typically petitioned for worldly favors such as reward
for good performance in school or work, protection on trips, or
for success toward a building's purpose at its dedication. Before
Kami are consulted the associated people, objects, and places are
ritualistically made clean through a process called O Harae. O
Harae is performed with the help of a Shinto priest, who directs
various rituals involving washing with water, the sprinkling of
salt, or the shaking of onusa, wooden wands with paper streamers
attached.

Kami are separated from the human world symbolically by
a torii (gate), which traditionally is made from two horizontal

supports born by two vertical supports, all painted red. Torii can be large works of architecture or small enough to sit on a desktop; all sizes are religiously significant. Torii mark the entrance to Shinto shrines, but the use of natural environment to complement the human element of proper protocol characterizes the shrine experience as a whole.

Shinto puts emphasis on successful living, and has little to say of an afterlife. Yomi, the land of the dead, is taught as the likely destination of all deceased. It is described as a gloomy, boring, resting place for spirits.

Cosmology

Shinto acknowledges a pantheon of specific divine personalities in addition to other, less differentiated kami. Amaterasu, the Sun Goddess, has a tie to the lineage of the Imperial Household of Japan as well as a connection to the Imperial Regalia of Japan. These Three Sacred Treasures - a sword, a jewel, and a mirror – have recorded history dating them as over one-thousand years old and are material objects representative of Japan's status as a spiritual protectorate under kami.

Syncretism

Japanese tend to view religion in a pragmatic way, and typically see no conflict in exploiting only the best parts of various religions. An example of this is the custom of overworked students to pray at Shinto shrines before exams. These same Japanese might later look to Christian churches to perform marriages, because they like the idea of God blessing a marriage. On another occasion a Buddhist temple would be sought to perform a funeral, because Buddhists are thought to have the most pleasant things to say about death and rebirth. Whatever other religious traditions are celebrated, the kami are always there to help when asked.

Scientology

Scientology Logo

Introduction

Scientology is a controversial religion that focuses on people as immortal beings who have fallen off of the correct path. Using a system called auditing, members work through problematic events in their lives to become spiritually liberated. Although exact numbers are difficult to determine, the church estimates the number of practitioners to be about 15 million worldwide.

History

Scientology was founded by L. Ron Hubbard, incorporating his earlier work with a practice called Dianetics. Hubbard was a science fiction writer, who quickly garnered supporters when he released his book "Dianetics: The Modern Science of Mental Health." In 1951 Hubbard designed the "E-meter," the tool used by members as an auditing aid. One year later, Hubbard wrote the specific teachings of Scientology, and in 1954 supporters of Hubbard created a Church of Scientology in California. After this the religion grew quickly, spreading to other countries such as Britain, Australia, and South Africa.

L. Ron Hubbard was one of the most instrumental people in shaping Scientology; however there were others who played significant roles. Dr. Joseph Winter worked with Hubbard to have Scientology accepted by the medical community. Some of Scientology's biggest supporters are celebrities. Hubbard himself encouraged celebrities to join the religion, even creating "Project

Celebrity," a list of famous people he asked to join the religion. Current celebrity members include Tom Cruise, Katie Holmes, Marie Presley, Kirstie Alley, and John Travolta.

Beliefs / Spirituality

Scientology is as complex as any religion. The main belief involves the thetan, an individual's life force. This is believed to be a person's real identity. It is believed that thetans fell off their path when they became too involved with their creative creations, rather than their spiritual nature. As time went on, thetans became only beings, losing their memory of their former selves. In Scientology, thetans are reborn many times, similar to reincarnation. Those in the religion are attempting to fully develop their spiritual selves and gain freedom. This is accomplished by making donations to the church and receiving materials and audits to further their growth. The process of this spiritual growth is called the Bridge.

Controversy

Controversy surrounds Scientology, with many scientists and governments claiming it is nothing but science fiction at best, and a cult at worst. In areas outside the United States, Scientology does not receive tax-exempt status as a religion, and is viewed with skepticism. It is continually questioned.

Sikhism

The Khanda

There is only one breath. All are made of the same clay. The light within all is the same.
- Guru Granth Sahib, page 96

Introduction

Sikhism was a religion founded in the northwestern Indian subcontinent through a revelation from Almighty God to Nanak (born 1469 CE), who gained the title Guru (teacher). Guru Nanek appointed a successor, as did each in a line of successors. By the early 1700s it was known that there would not be another human Guru, but rather the book Guru Granth Sahib would act as perpetual Guru thenceforth.

Sikhism has an unusual undercurrent of thought in assuming that one's religion might be an unchosen matter of birth as it relates to geography or era, and therefore one is only partially responsible for participating in it. By this circumvention of elitism the Sikhs traditionally establish a magnanimous sense of brotherhood between themselves and other faith traditions.

Sikhs accept concepts of karma and reincarnation but teach that Almighty God ultimately grants salvation. Descriptions of places such as "heaven" or "hell" in this scheme have little meaning.

Brotherhood

Sikhism stands out as a social movement as well as a religion. Sikhs strive to treat all people equally, regardless of religion, gender, social status, or any other factor commonly used to enforce discrimination.

While Sikhs personally value their religious beliefs over all others, they recognize that their personal beliefs may not be equally valuable to others. Sikhs claim that there are multiple ways to please Almighty God, and that they themselves are but one group of God's children. Almighty God offers salvation on some other basis than perfunctory choice of religion.

Five K's

Sikhs themselves stand out instantly in public by five outward signs, these being:

1. Kesh (uncut hair), often wrapped in a turban
2. Kanga (comb), to keep hair neat
3. Kara (steel bracelet), worn on dominant arm
4. Kirpan (sword), usually small, a reminder of freedom
5. Kaccha (breeches), which actually are often not publicly displayed

Each of these articles is related to Sikh values as taught by the Gurus. Note that during youth, Sikhs typically are casual about displaying these signs. After an initiation with Amrit (holy water) the Sikh is considered Khalsa. Anyone undergoing this ceremony chooses Sikhism over other faith systems.

Authority

Sikhs have neither priestly class nor central religious authority. There is an organization called the Shiromani Gurdwara Prabandhak Committee (SGPC) who are responsible for civil matters relating to the upkeep of Sikhism as a religion; it also is a political entity for the Sikhs as a nation. Leaders in the SGPC are democratically elected.

The Harmandir Sahib (Golden Temple) in Amritsar, Punjab, is the most culturally and historically significant Sikh religious center; however, all places which contain the Guru Granth Sahib are equally worthy of being a place of worship.

Spiritism

Allan Kardec

Introduction

Established in France in the nineteenth century, Spiritism is often referred to as French Spiritualism. It has since spread through many countries including the United States, Canada, Spain, Japan, Germany, and England. Currently, Brazil has the largest number of followers of any country. In general, the idea of Spiritism is a belief in the existence of spirits, and has been influenced by other fundamental world religions.

History

Spiritism began as a result of events seen and experienced by Allan Kardec who believed he was witnessing the work of spirits. The writings of this Frenchman, about a communication with spirits, was expanded and further established by other well-known writers. Arthur Conan Doyle, Johannas Greber, and Ernesto Bozzano were fundamental in the creation of this spiritual practice. Kardec himself states that much of his ideas behind Spiritism came from such important philosophical and religious leaders as Socrates, Plato, Francis of Assisi and even Jesus of Nazareth.

Structure

Quite unusual from other practices such as this, Spiritism does not proclaim itself to be a religion. No membership or organized following is necessary, and this practice seems to be more intellectual and spiritual than strictly religious. "Followers" of

Spiritism participate in regular bi-weekly or tri-weekly meetings, youth and children meetings, healings, lectures, book fairs, and Spiritist Week.

Beliefs & Spirituality

The doctrine of Spiritism, an interesting combination of spiritual concepts from Christianity, Positivism, and Platonism, is outlined in numerous books. Spiritism has five main points of doctrine followed by some further beliefs in relation to Jesus, evolution, karma, and communications with the spiritual world.

Spiritism states that there is a God over all as well as spirits who have the ability to improve and perfect themselves. Spirits perfect themselves through gradual reincarnation, while communication and interfering in the lives of human beings. It is also said that life exists on other planets beside the earth.

Today

This non-religion spiritual life has received some criticism since the World Wars, though it certainly does not gain as much negative attention as other fundamental world religions. For the most part, Spiritism has been attacked very little perhaps due to being a relatively unknown spiritual practice.

Spiritism lives on in modern culture, seen in a number of movies, television programs, and soap operas. Perhaps some mentionable titles including Spiritism are The Sixth Sense, Passengers, and Ghost Whisperers. Because Brazil claims the largest numbers of Spiritists, the country also broadcasts four soap operas which include Spiritism as part of the plot line.

Taoism

Taijitu, or Yin-Yang

The Tao [way] that can be taught is not the eternal Tao.
- Lao-zi. ca 600-530 BCE

Introduction

Taoism, also known as Daosim, emphasizes harmony between humans and the natural world. It is a religion native to China and dating from 550 BCE – 400 BCE. Lao-zi, whose name means "Old Boy," is the purported founder of Taoism. His book, Dao de Jing (Classic of Tao), is simultaneously a powerful and ambiguous work containing phrasing with multiple meanings in its expounding of issues such as ethics, cosmology, epistemology, politics, and spiritual and material fulfilment.

The Chinese word "tao" means "way," and Taoism is a system which promises to teach the best way to do all things. To practitioners, the fact that its date of founding and its founder are lightly recorded in history is trivial. Taoism specifies no belief in an Almighty God but does assume sentient spiritual beings. It emphasizes right actions but does not proscribe many beliefs.

The Way

Following the Tao means making choices that are most wholesome, most natural, and most beneficial. The Tao is without purpose; its followers react to situations without having specific expectations or desires to mold them. An analogy from the Dao de Jing is that one should seek to resemble an uncarved stone. Where Western tradition argues about varying degrees of free will versus destiny, Taoism teaches that neither are significant and that humankind should live in a constant state of full and untapped potential.

The Universal Life Church Ministries

Qi, The Force

Tao spiritual tradition describes an all-pervasive force called qi (Chi), which means energy or breath. Qi itself has two states, one corresponding to inhalation (yin) and one to exhalation (yang). By this metaphor the connectedness of other opposites can explained; the proper balance of anything is the Tao as there is a correct ratio of all coexisting opposites which are necessary for the sustenance of life. Examples of other opposites include male and female; activity and rest; hot and cold.

There might be ways to harness qi and use it to enact material-world changes; the holistic health philosophy of Tai Chi refers to this power in its very name, as does the fullness of its martial tradition Tai Chi Chuan. Feng Shui is a system of material-world organization which permits qi to flow and eddy throughout a particular location without becoming stagnant and deleterious. Acupuncture and other Chinese medical traditions regulate the ebb, flow, and balance of qi. All of these practices stem from traditions dating back thousands of years, but none of these have been universally popular or systematically practiced throughout that entire time span.

Spirituality

Taoism most readily differentiates from Confucianism, its geographic and cultural neighbor, by its emphasis on spirituality. Ancestor veneration in Taoism is believed to bring auspicious divine intervention more than simple self-betterment.

Authority

Taoism is not associated with any institution or authority; in fact, most practitioners have incorporated Taoist traditions into their lives without separating their cultural traditions from the Taoist faith traditions. Taoism is a part of Chinese folk tradition and has an open canon. It is being and will continue to be adapted to changes associated with each generation.

Tenrikyo

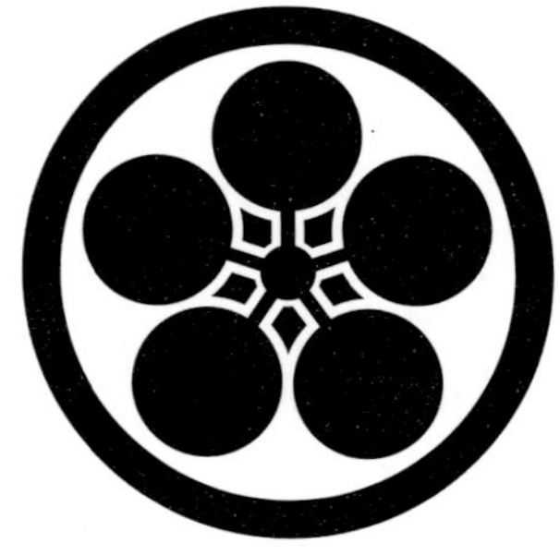

Tenrikyo Emblem

Introduction

Tenrikyo is a Japanese religion with about two million followers today, most of whom live in Japan. It is a newer religion, having been founded in the 19th century by a woman, Miki Nakayama. It is a monotheistic religion which believes that God, or Tenri-O-no-Mikoto, revealed wisdom through Nakayama and certain other people. Although reincarnation is part of Tenrikyo, its practitioners focus on cultivating worldly happiness, known as the Joyous Life, through charitable acts and kindness towards others.

History

Miki Nakayama founded Tenrikyo in 1838, when she felt the presence of Tenri-O-no-Mikoto while assisting in a Buddhist exorcism meant to cure her husband of illness. Nakayama began to teach Tenrikyo to others, including another person, Izo Iburi, who also received revelatory messages from Tenri-O-no-Mikoto and did much to spread Tenrikyo, as well as compile his and Nakayama's messages into formal texts. Government pressure forced Tenrikyo to become absorbed as a Buddhist sect for a while, but was later recognized by the Japanese government as a sect of Shinto, despite having a different theological nature than the polytheistic Shinto faith. Tenrikyo distinguished itself at this time due to its followers' humanitarian acts, such as founding orphanages and schools for the blind. After World War II, Tenrikyo practitioners asked the government to remove it from its status as Shinto sect, and Tenrikyo then got rid of much of its Buddhist and Shinto influence, although

The Universal Life Church Ministries

it still has retained some aspects of traditional Japanese worship practices. Today, a lack of political restrictions on Tenrikyo has allowed it to flourish in conventional society.

Spirituality

Followers of Tenrikyo hold God to be an entirely benevolent creator, who allows reincarnation but encourages the happiness of mankind during their mortal lives. To this end, Tenrikyo practitioners attempt to follow the path of the Joyous Life, which involves charity and mercy to others, and rejection of negative actions that would come out of greed, anger, or arrogance. Practitioners believe in the continual construction of a better world through small acts of daily kindness. To this end, many Tenrikyo followers have founded or participate in disaster relief programs, orphanages, hospitals, and schools. Music is important in Tenrikyo, and instruments are played in both daily and monthly services, although the prayers said during these services can be performed on one's own, if one cannot attend a temple at that time. Many followers of Tenrikyo also hold tenets of Christian or Buddhist beliefs.

Unitarian Universalism

Flaming Chalice

Introduction

Unitarian Universalism is a religious denomination which embraces theological diversity. It reflects the merger of two long-standing traditions: Unitarianism and Universalism. Both traditions have Judeo-Christian roots extending back hundreds of years; some even to the very beginnings of Christianity. Unitarian Universalism has no creed; its adherents are free to follow many paths in the search for truth and decide their own beliefs about theological issues.

History

Originally, Unitarians were simply Christians who did not believe in the Trinity. Instead, they advocated the unity of God as their founding doctrine. Unitarian beliefs have been part of Christian theology since the time of the death of Jesus. However, religious groups did not form around this theological principle until the 15th and 16th centuries in Europe. Unitarianism emerged in America in the early 19th century, primarily in New England in Congregationalist churches. The churches were organized around broad principles of rational thinking, the humanity of Jesus, and each individual having a direct relationship with God.

Universalism has an equally long history which extends deeply into the history of Christianity beginning with some of the earliest Church scholars such as Origen and St. Gregory of Nyssa. Universalists denounced the doctrine of eternal damnation in favor of universal salvation and a loving God who will redeem all.

The Universal Life Church Ministries

Universalism formed as a distinct denomination in America in 1793. Unitarians became a denomination in 1825. The two denominations consolidated into one, known as the Unitarian Universalist Association, in 1961. Today, there are approximately 1,041 congregations in Canada, the United States, and abroad. Worldwide membership is estimated at between 120,000 and 600,000 individuals.

Historically, both Unitarians and Universalists have been active in social justice, social reform, and other political issues. Their members have been involved in causes such as abolitionism, women's suffrage, civil rights, the feminist movement, gay rights, and other social reform campaigns.

<u>Spirituality</u>

Unitarian Universalism's defining characteristic is that it has no set beliefs. While both traditions began as divergent groups within Christianity and looked to the Bible as their source of truth, today the organization recognizes sacred texts and scriptures from all religions. There is no one way to think about the soul, the afterlife, or even God. While welcomed, belief in God is not required to be a member of a congregation. A variety of spiritual practices are found and welcomed within the congregations: Humanist, Agnostic, Earth-centered, Atheist, Buddhist, Christian and Pagan are the most prevalent.

Zoroastrianism

"Now the two primal Spirits, who reveal themselves in vision as Twins, are the Better and the Bad, in thought and word and action. Between these two the wise ones chose aright; the foolish not so."
-Avesta: Yasna 30 Ahunavaiti Gatha, verse 3

Faravahar

Introduction

Zoroastrianism is a religion founded in Persia (Iran) by Zoroaster (Zarathushtra) sometime between 1200-600 BCE. It is a religion which promised salvation in exchange for right belief based on the teachings of a closed religious canon; historically, however, many original scriptures were lost when Iskandar (Alexander the Great) attacked Darius III's Persian Empire in 330 BCE.

It is a faith system which treats human devotion to asha (truth and righteousness) as the necessary precondition to bring about Ahura Mazda's (Almighty God's) destruction of evil.

Cosmology

Ahura Mazda created the universe from nothing and made humankind desirous of good but ignorant of asha, the truth. There is something profound and valuable about the act of seeking asha; furthermore, it is within the ability of humankind to do so.

There is a foil to Ahura Mazda's infinite goodness, and it is a finite evil entity or lie named Angre Mainyu. These two entities also have a set of spiritual underlings, Mazda's being the ahuras and Angre Mainyu's being the daevas (compare Vedic Hindu tradition, which reverses these roles). Mithra is the leader of the ahuras, and is like a leader of an angelic order.

The Universal Life Church Ministries

Salvation

The Avesta is the primary collection of sacred texts of Zoroastrianism and it charges readers to seek asha. It teaches that, upon simple reflection, one should realize that Ahura Mazda is good and that humankind is integral and potent in the overcoming of Angre Mainyu. The start of this battle between moral spirits is in finding wisdom; upon prayerful request, Mazda will aid His devotees to that end.

Mazda typically executes His spiritual designs for humans through Fravashi, or guardian angels. This is comparable to His executing His material world plans through humans themselves. Ultimately, human efforts will banish evil and unrighteousness from the material world.

Afterlife

There is a judgment for humans to determine residence in one of two spiritual planes in the afterlife. After death, a person crosses the Bridge of the Separator and enters either the Abode of Songs and exists in asha; otherwise a person enters the House of Lies and exists without asha.

Culture

During the Islamic conquest of Persia around 650 CE many Zoroastrians were displaced to India, where Zoroastrianism lives today through the Parsis and Iranis in India as well as the communities who stayed in Iran. Despite geographical separation for an extended period of time, most members of Zoroastrian faith remained true to its precepts and today the religion is not formally sectarian.

Zoroastrian culture teaches equality of all humans regardless of born traits or religion. Environmental concerns are historically also a cultural devotion.

Appendix – Our Universal Beliefs

Life Is...

Freedom

Freedom is the most important thing to everyone. Every living thing fights for its freedom – freedom to shape its own destiny, freedom of movement, freedom to fulfill its dreams and ambitions so long as that pursuit does not infringe on the rights and freedoms of others. Some would say our Creator endows us all with this inalienable right. Others posit that it defies the natural order for any human to have dominion over another. Regardless of its theological or philosophical underpinnings, the belief in freedom has borne up countless struggles for good and justice throughout the ages. Such freedom is a core tenet of the Universal Life Church Monastery, an end to which we tirelessly advocate.

Food

Without food there can be no freedom, only a desperate fight for survival. Thus food is key and fundamental to prosperity and happiness for all humankind. There is enough soil, water, and sunlight on this planet that under responsible stewardship, no mouth should go unfed, and no thirst unquenched. We dedicate ourselves to the task of alleviating hunger and malnutrition throughout the world. When people see beyond the immediacy of day-to-day survival, great thoughts, ideas and futures can flourish.

Sexuality

Sexuality is essential to the continuation of the human race. For years, societies have feared sex and maligned expressions of sexuality that were not for the purpose of procreation. We are born with sexual instincts. These should be neither stifled nor condemned. In much the same way as the pursuit of freedom must be held in check by the consideration of its externalities, sexuality should have no other requirement than that it is devoid of coercion and exploitation. Sex should be celebrated as a positive force, not hidden under a bushel. To deny our natural desires or feel ashamed of our instinctive urges is to deny life itself.

Glossary of Terms

Almighty God
The name for a single God who created the universe from nothing, and who is omniscient, omnipotent, and by definition benevolent. Respectfully this name is used as the English translation to describe any such being.

BCE / CE
Terminology now standard in world media corresponding to the calendar system. 1 CE, meaning year 1 of the Common Era, refers to the year of the birth of Jesus of Nazareth. 1 BCE, meaning 1 year before the Common Era, refers to the year immediately before the birth of Jesus of Nazareth.

Canon
Ideas, almost always in text, which exist in a permanent form and which define a religion.

Divinity
A sentient spiritual entity.

Enlightenment
A profound ability to make correct assessments and right decisions.

Faith
Belief in the absence of proof, supported by evidence which is not universally recognized.

Spirit
The opposite of material; anything which exists but cannot be measured with methods used in physical science (physics).